Contents

CAMBRIDGE
UNIVERSITY PRESS

CAMBRIDGE UNIVERSITY PRESS
Cambridge, New York, Melbourne, Madrid, Cape Town, Singapore, São Paulo

Cambridge University Press
The Edinburgh Building, Cambridge CB2 8RU, UK

www.cambridge.org
Information on this title: www.cambridge.org/9780521704755

First published 2007

Printed in the United Kingdom at the University Press, Cambridge

A catalogue record for this publication is available from the British Library

ISBN 978-0-521-70475-5 paperback

ACKNOWLEDGEMENTS

Cover
Marek Jagucki

Artwork
The Best Reader in the Whole World: Marek Jagucki
Grandpa John: Jackie Stafford-Snider
This is the Mum: Jackie Stafford-Snider
Please Send Back the Baby: Rob Loxston, Lemonade Illustration

Texts
'The Best Reader in the Whole World' by Gordon Askew; 'Please Send Back the Baby' by Jane Clarke; 'Grandpa John' reproduced by permission of The Agency (London) Ltd © 1987 Tony Bradman. First published by Viking Press. All rights reserved and enquiries to The Agency (London) Ltd, 24 Pottery Lane, London W11 4LZ fax: 0207 727 9037; 'This is the Mum' reproduced by permission of The Agency (London) Ltd © 1988 Tony Bradman. First published by Viking Press. All rights reserved and enquiries to The Agency (London) Ltd, 24 Pottery Lane, London W11 4LZ fax: 0207 727 9037

Layout and typesetting by eMC Design Ltd, www.emcdesign.org.uk

The Best Reader in the Whole World

Gordon Askew

Ben wanted his mum to read his favourite book to him.

His mum was the best reader in the whole world. She knew all the names and could do all the different voices.

When she read the funny bits, Ben grinned and giggled.

When she read the silky streams of words, Ben felt snuggly inside.

But …

… on Saturday, things were different.

Ben longed for his mum to read to him …
but she wasn't there.

Ben found his dad instead.

Dad was busy decorating. There was paint and wallpaper everywhere.

Ben held out the book.

"Please will you read to me?"

But Dad read too fast.

He didn't say the names properly and he couldn't do all the voices.

It just wasn't the same.

At teatime, Ben found his gran. She was almost hidden in a blur of wool and clicking needles.

Ben held out his book.

"Please will you read to me?"

Gran read beautifully. But when she got to the funny bits, Ben didn't chortle at all.

It just wasn't the same.

At bedtime, Ben went to find his grandpa. There he was, struggling to put something together.

Ben held out his book and gave
Grandpa his sweetest smile.

"Please will you read to me?"

Grandpa tried very hard. But when he came to the silky streams of words, his voice was rough and didn't flow.

It just wasn't the same.

The next day, Mum came back. She brought a milky bundle with her. It wailed and smelled disgusting.

Ben held out his book.

"Read to me!" he demanded.

"Oh Ben! You can see
I'm busy with Kate,"
Mum protested.

So Ben found Zengo instead.

"You'll read to me, won't you?"

Zengo tried his best, but it just wasn't the same.

Then Ben's mum whispered, "Your new sister is asleep now. Come here and I'll read to you."

Ben felt all snuggly inside.

His mum really was the best reader in the whole world.

Questions

Discuss these questions with the child/children as you read through the book together.

- Who do you think is the best reader in the whole world? Why? (title page)
- How do we know Ben thinks his mum is the *best reader in the whole world*? What clues can you find? (page 7)
- What do you think *silky streams of words* means? What other words could we use instead of 'silky'? (e.g. smooth, flowing, soft, etc.) (page 7)
- How do you think Ben feels when he feels *snuggly inside*? What other words could we use instead of 'snuggly'? (e.g. warm, happy, comfortable, safe, etc.) (page 7)
- How do you think Ben feels when his mum reads to him? Why? (page 7)
- How do you think Ben feels when his mum isn't there? What makes you think this? (page 8)
- How do you think Ben feels when his dad reads to him? Why? (page 11)
- What does it mean for Gran to be *hidden in a blur of wool and clicking needles*? What is she doing, and how? (page 12)

- How do you think Ben feels when his gran reads to him? Why? (page 14)
- How do you think Ben feels when his grandpa reads to him? Why? (page 17)
- How do you think Ben feels when his mum comes home with his sister Kate? What makes you think this? How would you feel if you were Ben? (page 18)
- How does Mum read? (does different voices, makes Ben laugh, makes him feel snuggly inside) Which of these things would be most important to you? Why? (page 23)
- What do you think is the most important thing to do when you are reading aloud? What do you enjoy when someone reads to you? (page 23)
- Which words would you use to describe Ben's mum? What do you think she would be like if you met her? (page 23)
- What words would you use to describe Ben? What do you think he would be like if you met him? (page 23)
- Where do you think the author might have got his idea for this story? (page 23) Why do you think this?
- What do the illustrations tell us about the characters and how they are feeling?

Hometime

Poems about families

Grandpa John

Grandpa John
Is nice to me;
Sits me on his
Bony knees.

Tickles my chin,
Tweaks my nose,
Tells me I'm his
Little rose.

Grandpa John
Gives me some money,
Tells me I'm
His little honey.

Reads me stories,
Sings me songs;
Tells me I'm
Where I belong.

Tony Bradman

This is the Mum

This is the mum
Who wakes me up
And gets me out of bed

This is the mum
Who helps me pull
My clean vest over my head

This is the mum
Who irons my clothes
Who puts out my clean socks

This is the mum
Who puts my lunch
Inside my new lunchbox

This is the mum
Who goes to work
Who tries not to be late

This is the mum
Who stands in the rain
By the Infant gate

This is the mum
Who later on
Is there to make my tea

This is the mum
Who's looking tired
And occasionally

This is the mum
Who tells me off
For gobbling my food

This is the mum
Who loses her temper
When I'm being rude

This is the mum
Who loves me
At least that's what
  she said

And this is the mum
Who's telling me
To get myself to bed

Tony Bradman

Please Send Back the Baby

Please send back the baby,
You can see it doesn't work.
All it does is lie there,
It's driving me berserk.

I want one I can play with
That will not yell or leak.
You said I must be patient,
But we've had it for a week.

It's time to get our money back,
I'm sure you will agree.
So please send back the baby,
While it's under guarantee.

Jane Clarke

Questions

Discuss these questions with the child/children as you read through the book together.

- What do you know about Grandpa John? (page 28)
- What words does the poet use to describe Grandpa John? (page 28)
- Does Grandpa John remind you of anyone you know? Who, and why? (page 29)
- What does the child in the poem think of Grandpa John? (page 29)
- What does Grandpa John think of the child? (page 29)
- Do you think the poet is talking about one mum, or lots of different mums? (page 35)
- What question would you like to ask Tony Bradman about his poem? (page 35)
- How does the older child feel? How do you know? (page 38)

- Who do you think the older child is talking to in this poem? Why do you think that? (page 38)
- What does the child mean by *it doesn't work*? (page 36)
- What does the child mean when he or she talks about how the baby *leaks*? (page 37)
- Which of the three poems was the funniest? What made it funny? (page 38)
- Which of the three poems was your favourite? What made it your favourite? (page 38)